★ ★ ★ ★ ★ ★ ★ ★ ★ ★ ★ ★

NITRO CIRCUS

BEST OF BMX

RIPLEY

PUBLISHING

a Jim Pattison Company

BMX: DREAM THE EXTREME!
A MIX OF MOTOCROSS, CYCLING, AND SKATEBOARDING TRICKS!

BMX stands for "bicycle motocross." BMX racing is a cycling sport originally inspired by motocross racing. Young cyclists saw how much fun the motocross bikers were having and wanted to create their own extreme races. Some riders added tricks, whips, and flips inspired by skateboarders, and freestyle BMX was born!

BMX racing dates back to the late 1960s and early 1970s in California when young riders raced their small-framed, "ape-hanger" handlebar bikes along dirt tracks. The first national BMX race was held in 1974. In just a few years, riders were flipping, riding half-pipes, and pulling tricks off handrails. Nowadays, competitors participate either in BMX racing, freestyle BMX, or BMX big air, which is one of the flagship events for the Summer X Games and Nitro World Games competitions.

BMX racing became a medal sport at the 2008 Summer Olympics in Beijing.

Freestyle BMX is stunt riding on a bike. It will be part of the Olympic Games for the first time in 2020!

BMX bikes are usually made of steel or aluminum. Bike wheels vary from 16″ to 26″ in size.

Freestyle BMX riders love to master air tricks and flatland tricks!

BMX bikes come in many different varieties, but they all have small frames, a single gear, thick tires, and high handlebars, for extra comfort.

Freestyle BMX is considered one of the most extreme action sports because of its high degree of risk and danger. The speed, height, and difficulty of the moves all make it an exhilarating and dangerous experience!

FREESTYLE TRICKS VERSUS RACING SPEED

FROM SPEED, TO TRICKS, TO AIR!

BMX racing is off-road sprint racing inspired by motocross. Riders race around a one-lap course that includes dirt jumps, rolling hills, and steeply banked turns. The BMX race is all about speed. As many as eight riders line up at the starting gate to race. Because of the speed and the difficulty of the course, multiple-bike pileups are common.

Vert riders use a half-pipe ramp structure to perform air tricks while going side to side along the ramp. BMX vert has been featured in every Summer X Games competition since 1995.

Dirt jumping evolved alongside BMX racing but involves riding over soil or dirt jumps. Dirt jumper bikes are a mix between a BMX bike and a mountain bike.

Freestyle BMX is stunt riding on a BMX bike. It evolved from BMX racing, was influenced by skateboarding, and is more about tricks and flips. Riders use rails, ramps, curbs, and trails, as well as their skill and creativity, to catch air and wow the audience. There are hundreds of freestyle BMX tricks, including the Superman, tire grab, toboggan, tailwhip, steamroller, footjam, and time machine, and more are invented every day!

Freestyle BMX has multiple disciplines: **vert, dirt, street, park, flatland, and big air.**

Flatland riders artistically spin, hop, and balance their bikes on smooth, flat surfaces.

Park (as in "skate park") riders use wooden or cement ramps to learn and master their tricks.

Street riders use public spaces and structures, such as curbs, rails, and stairs, to perform their tricks.

COMPETING ON THE GRAND STAGE

WINNING BMX GOLD!

A BMX racing competition involves multiple heats (or *motos*). They begin with qualifying rounds, and the winners move on to quarterfinals, semifinals, and the finals.

Freestyle BMX is one of the most-watched events of the Summer X Games action sports competition, and BMX vert (14' tall vertical quarter pipes linked by a 15' flat bottom) has been a part of the games since the beginning.

KEY FACTS

BMX racing is somewhat new to the Olympics and became a medal sport in 2008 during the Summer Olympics. There are both women's and men's BMX racing events, which are held over the course of three days.

The X Games is an annual action sports event that has been hosted, produced, and broadcast by ESPN since 1995. It awards medals to athletes in five areas of BMX freestyle (vert, park, street, big air, and dirt), BMX racing, and many other extreme sports, including skateboarding and mountain biking. There is also a yearly Winter X Games competition.

NITRO WORLD GAMES

At the 2017 Nitro World Games, Ryan Williams was the only athlete in the competition to make the finals in two events in two disciplines. Williams won in Scooter Best Trick and BMX Best Trick and was the first competitor to ever win multiple events at Nitro World Games.

NITRO WORLD GAMES

First held in 2016 and created by Nitro Circus, Nitro World Games is an international action sport competition. Athletes in BMX, FMX (freestyle motocross), scootering, inline skating, and skateboarding compete for medals. In just a few years, these games have seen many broken records and world firsts!

BMX BEST TRICK
JUNE 24 2017
SALT LAKE CITY, UT

FLAT

Flatland riders perform their tricks on smooth, flat surfaces (usually concrete). They don't use ramps or rails, but instead spin, hop, and balance on their bikes, with the goal of not touching the ground. They are judged by style and flow, the difficulty of their tricks, and showmanship. It's considered the most artistic form of freestyle BMX.

FREECOASTER HUB
These special hubs allow riders to move backward without having to pedal.

REAR & FRONT PEGS
Flatland bikes usually have front and back pegs, which allow riders to balance and shift weight to different positions by standing on the pegs.

WHEELBASE
The wheelbase is much shorter, making it easier to spin and do tricks.

LAND

FRAME
Flatland frames are low profile with a high bottom bracket for lots of maneuverability.

HANDLEBAR
Flatland bike handlebars are "zero-offset," which means they have the same position and feel whether they face forward or backward.

ROTORS
Rotors allow the handlebars to turn 360 degrees without the cables becoming entangled. Riders can do more spins and tricks with a rotor.

FRONT & REAR BRAKES
Flatland bikes often have front and rear brakes for maximum control over the bike.

TIRES
Flatland bikes use very high-pressure tires, so they roll smooth and fast.

FLATLAND BMX: LIKE DANCING ON A BIKE

BOUNCING, HOPPING, AND POPPING

TRICK #1

THE POGO

The pogo is a flatland BMX trick that requires balance and precision. It's basically hopping on one wheel only while standing on the pegs. You do this by applying the brakes and using your weight to bring the wheel off the ground.

Your weight, not your arms, should be pulling the wheel off the ground. You are using the bike like a pogo stick, bouncing up and down on one wheel. You must be good at endos and track stands before you can hope to master the pogo. Always keep the brakes applied during a pogo.

NITRO METER

BEGINNER · INTERMEDIATE · ADVANCED

KEY FACTS

Flatland riders bring expression and emotion into their tricks.

Flatland BMX is often compared to breakdancing because of its similar style and flow.

Flatland riders are very dedicated and disciplined, and flatland BMX takes lots of practice to do well.

Riders are also judged by how often their feet touch the ground during trick sequences. The fewer toe touches, the better.

TRACK STAND

Balance is the key to almost every BMX trick; the track stand, which is borrowed from track and road cycling, is a great way to learn how to control your bodyweight and your bike!

The track stand is basically balancing on your bike without moving anywhere. It's easiest to start by rolling slowly forward with your feet on the pedals and hands on the handlebars, then once you are balanced, squeeze your brake to stop moving. Remain stationary for as long as you can, and when you feel your weight shift too much to one side, pedal forward to regain your balance. Repeat by stopping for longer and longer each time until you can stay balanced for as long as you want!

BEGINNER · INTERMEDIATE · ADVANCED

NITRO METER

DIRT JUM

The dirt jumper is a mix of BMX and mountain bike types. It has a very sturdy frame and huge wheels with mega-knobby tires. Dirt jumper bikes are super versatile, and often hit the Giganta ramp at Nitro Circus shows.

SEAT

Seats are positioned low and out of the way, allowing for more space to maneuver your body during tricks.

BRAKES

Dirt jumpers, like most contemporary mountain bikes, use disc brakes. They provide better stopping power and more control.

DID YOU KNOW?

The small and compact frame of the dirt jumper makes it easer to move around in the air so riders can perform a wide variety of tricks.

FRAME

All dirt jumper frames are made of aluminum to be light and stiff.

SUSPENSION

Stiff front shocks help absorb the impact of landing from big air tricks while also allowing for control navigating around dirt tracks or skate parks.

TIRES

Their tires have the heaviest treads of all BMX bikes to carry riders through jumps and bumps. Wheel size is usually 26".

FREES

Freestyle BMX bikes have super sturdy frames, built for tricks and flips on several surfaces, including ramps, rails, and flat concrete. Freestyle bikes are a favorite of Nitro Circus riders and are used for big air competitions.

REAR BRAKES
Freestyle BMX bikes use U-brakes, but some riders prefer not to use any brakes at all.

FRAME
Frames are compact (usually 20.5–21.5") and very sturdy.

REAR & FRONT PEGS
Freestyle BMX bikes usually have front and rear pegs, which allow the riders to do special tricks and grind on rails and bars.

WHEELBASE
The wheelbase is very short, making it easier to spin the bike and do tricks.

ROTOR

Rotors allow the handlebars to turn in a 360 without the cables becoming entangled. Riders can do more spins and tricks with a rotor.

TIRES

Their high-pressure, usually nubby, tires have 36 spokes! The tread can differ, depending on where you spend your time doing tricks.

RIDE SAFE AND SMART!
FREESTYLE BMX SAFETY TIPS

Being safe means more time on your bike and less time laid up with injuries. Being safe isn't just about the right equipment—it's about riding safely, too. To start, don't ride above your ability—especially when you're learning new tricks and techniques. And always start with and master easier tricks before you move on to the advanced ones!

Be aware of your surroundings. Whether you're a street, vert, flatland, or dirt BMXer, you need to watch out for hazards. If you're a flatland or street rider, that might mean watching out for pedestrians or other traffic, or even trash, glass, and other hazards in the road.

Also check the track for any debris and potential issues before you ride. If you're a vert or park rider, your most likely hazard is the other riders. Follow the basic rules and make sure the ramps are clear of riders before you take off.

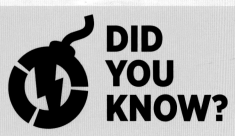

DID YOU KNOW?

It takes a long time and lots of practice to master the tricks you see top BMX freestyle riders doing. Start with the foundations, like the bunny hop, manual, and endo, before you try the insane combos.

Your BMX bike takes a beating when you're racing or mastering tricks. Make sure every part of your bike is tight before riding! Be sure to give your bike a once-over and check these parts:

1. Do your tires need air? Freestyle BMX tires should be pumped to their maximum allowance for best balance and bounce.

2. Make sure your brakes are working. Check the hand action and make sure it's making contact with the tires.

3. Make sure nothing is loose. The bumpy terrain or jarring jumps can loosen connections over time.

4. Make sure the seat is tightly fastened.

GEAR UP FOR BEST RESULTS

GO LONGER, FASTER, HIGHER, AND HAVE MORE FUN!

With freestyle BMX riding, it's not "if" but "when" you will fall. But if you have the right protective gear—that means a helmet, gloves, elbow pads, and kneepads—those falls won't faze you. Protective gear will mean you can try more sick tricks, feel safer while learning, keep going after a fall, and build your skills faster. Don't expect to fly through the air without some safety gear.

Top BMX freestyle riders always practice with safety gear. They know if they get hurt, they might not be able to compete. Most competitive BMX riders

1. Pick a strong, sturdy "skate" style helmet that has more protection for the back of the head. Make sure the helmet is CPSC certified so you know it will be strong and safe. Bell Helmets is one of the leading brands that most of the Nitro athletes wear.

2. Gloves prevent callouses from the bike grips and protect your hands from cement and asphalt when you fall. When you're not in constant pain, you'll have more fun.

to wear helmets, and the pros often wear full-face helmets, as commonly seen on BMX racing events. Experienced flatland BMX riders typically do not wear much protective gear, maybe because they don't

jump high or race at high speeds. But if you're just learning, you will fall, start with a helmet at least and save yourself a concussion!

PRO TIPS

NITRO CIRCUS MATTY WHYATT

Some skate parks and online organizations will donate proper helmets to riders if they can't afford them. Find an organization that will help you out. Also try second-hand sports stores, but make sure the helmet hasn't been damaged. Most of all, don't use a regular bike helmet!

3. Your elbows and knees are often the first things that hit the ground when a trick goes wrong. Protect them so you can be up and riding in no time!

4. Wear closed-toe shoes that have good grips on the soles so that you don't slip off the pedals.

START WITH THE BASICS
BUILDING A FOUNDATION

In freestyle BMX, there are a few basic skills that are essential to learning everything else, no matter how crazy the combo!

You have to start by mastering these important and fundamental techniques, as they are the building blocks that you need to become a master at freestyle in all its forms!

BUNNY HOP

TRICK #3

NITRO METER

BEGINNER · INTERMEDIATE · ADVANCED · CRAZY!!

LEARNING THE BUNNY HOP!

Start by riding along with your feet level on the pedals and practice pulling your handlebars to your waist. Work on that until you can get your crossbar up to your chest. Then, add on by pulling even harder and jumping straight up using your legs.

Jump your body at the same time as you pull the handlebars. The more you practice, the higher and more controlled your bunny hop will become.

TRICK #4

THE MANUAL

Freestyle riders use the manual to tie two tricks together in a sequence.

A manual is when you're riding on the rear wheel and not turning your pedals. Riding at medium speed, lift the front wheel off the ground, shift your body weight backward—with your back and abdomen rigid—and balance with your legs.

BEGINNER INTERMEDIATE ADVANCED

NITRO METER

PRO TIPS

NITRO CIRCUS

TODD MEYN

Don't fear the manual. Especially since BMX bikes are so small and close to the ground, your chances of falling backward are much less likely than you think. Start in the grass. If you fear falling backward. One leg will naturally come to the ground and stop you from falling too far back.

Once you have the fundamental techniques firmly in hand, you can start building on them, creating your own style, and displaying amazing combos. Now you have a toolbox of tricks to start building with!

DOUBLE PEG GRIND

After choosing a railing or ledge a little higher than your pegs, ride up to it and do a side hop (sideways bunny hop) onto it—landing right on the pegs and bending your arms and legs for cushion—stay balanced as you grind along the railing. As you slow down, bunny hop off the rail and you're done!

BEGINNER INTERMEDIATE ADVANCED CRAZY

NITRO METER

THE FOOT JAM

To do the foot jam, stop your front wheel against a curb or wall (or use the front brake to stop) and then lift your back wheel up high, while maintaining control.

BEGINNER INTERMEDIATE ADVANCED

NITRO METER

ROUND AND ROUND THEY GO!

SPINNING IN THE AIR

Aerial spins come in many shapes and sizes and are some of the most important air tricks in freestyle BMX riding. You make the entire bike spin around while in the air. These are measured in degrees, such as 180, 360 (one full rotation), 540, 720, and even 900 (that's two-and-a-half times around)!

To get good at spins, you need to be comfortable approaching your jumps at moderate speeds. Then start with the 360-degree spin and build from there. The 180-degree spin can sometimes be harder because you'll be landing and riding out of the spin backward (called a *fakie*)! Note that if you ride right foot forward, you will spin to your left, and if you ride left foot forward, you will spin to the right.

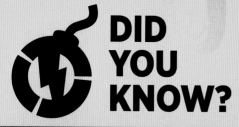

DID YOU KNOW?

A barspin is when you spin the handlebars around while the front tire (or the whole bike) is airborne and then catch the handlebars in the forward position. Flatland BMXers also perform this trick in combinations with other flatland techniques.

TRUCK DRIVER

The truck driver is a good example of how freestyle riders combine several tricks together into combos to make their tricks more impressive and harder to copy.

The truck driver is an aerial spin where you spin the bike 360 degrees while doing a barspin (a.k.a. when you spin the handlebars around while the front tire, or the whole bike, is airborne and then catch the handlebars in the forward position) at the same time. Wherever you turn your head and shoulders, your body will want to go naturally. As long as your head and shoulders are spinning, the rest of your body will follow.

BEGINNER INTERMEDIATE ADVANCED CRAZY!

NITRO METER

PRO TIPS

**NITRO CIRCUS
ANDY BUCKWORTH**

As you get more comfortable doing various spins, you can add to the complexity of the spin by doing one-hand, no-hand, and one-foot spins. The pros do just that to create combos of spins and flips that no one has ever seen before!

TABLETOP

What is the tabletop? While in the air, you bring the bike up to one side of your body by turning the handlebars and using your body to flatten the bike like the top of a table.

The tabletop is often confused with the invert trick, which is harder and does not include as much turning of the bars, but still executes the move into a tabletop.

Enter the jump with good speed, and then at the peak height of the jump, your right knee (if you ride right foot forward) crosses over the frame and pushes down while your other leg pulls up. This causes the bike to flatten out.

NITRO METER

BEGINNER INTERMEDIATE ADVANCED

THE INVERT

PRO TIPS

NITRO CIRCUS
KURTIS DOWNS

Learn to visualize a trick from start to finish, then take it step by step until you complete your goal. Practicing the movements on the ground before doing them in the air is key. Remember to always keep your knees together during the tabletop and invert.

The invert is an extended upside-down tabletop and a much harder trick!

The tabletop is considered an intermediate level trick, whereas the invert is considered an advanced level one.

DID YOU KNOW?

An **air** is any trick you do while in the air. Once you feel comfortable with fast, controlled jumps, start with bar turns and barspins and build from there.

NITRO METER

BEGINNER INTERMEDIATE ADVANCED

COOL AIR TRICKS TO START WITH

THE ONE-FOOT AND CAN-CAN: YOU CAN!

TRICK #10

TUCK NO-HANDER

You take your hands off the bars and tuck the bars into your lap!

Riding at an easy speed, do a regular jump at a decent height, pulling the handlebars toward your waist and bending your knees slightly at the peak of the jump. During each attempt, try to pull up the handlebars earlier, squeezing the bike frame to hold it in place. If you feel the bike wobbling or the handlebars turning, you need to hold the bike better.

THE CAN-CAN

TRICK #11

The can-can is where you bring the dominant foot completely over the bike to the other side and then return it to the pedal before landing.

Going further, the no-footed can-can is when the rider does a can-can but also takes the other foot off the pedal, so that both legs are on one side of the bike and both feet are off the pedals.

NITRO METER

BEGINNER · INTERMEDIATE · ADVANCED · CRAZY!

PRO TIPS

Make sure you know which foot is forward during your jumps because this will determine which side you use to enter, lead, and pull off a trick. Don't forget that BMX tricks can be performed on other types of bikes, like the dirt jumper pictured here.

NITRO CIRCUS
ETHAN ROBERTS

DON'T FEAR THE LOOKBACK!

LOOKING BACK

TRICK #12

TURNDOWN

While in the air, the rider pulls the handlebars up and pushes the bike out with the legs, towards his rear, nondominant foot.

NITRO METER

BEGINNER · INTERMEDIATE · ADVANCED · CRAZY

NITRO CIRCUS
MATTY WHYATT

PRO TIPS

Make sure you know which is your dominant side when you ride. If you ride right foot forward, the right's your dominant side. It affects which way you spin and turn.

THE LOOKBACK

This intermediate trick is a great one to use to connect two other tricks, as a transition.

At the height of the jump, you twist the handlebars down and to the right (if you ride right foot forward), while at the same time pushing the bike straight out to the same side of the body using your legs.

NITRO METER

BEGINNER INTERMEDIATE ADVANCED CRAZY

DID YOU KNOW?

This trick is a combination of an opposite air and a turndown. It's sometimes used to make a higher-skilled transfer or turn in a quarter pipe.

PRO TIPS

NITRO CIRCUS
JAIE TOOHEY

Start by doing an opposite air (your nondominant side), then do a turndown right before you reach midair. You should land facing forward.

UP, UP, AND AWAY!

LEARN TO FLY LIKE SUPERMAN!

As you get more comfortable doing the Superman, you'll be able to stretch out and extend your legs more. The bigger the air, the more time you have to extend and add variations, such as the KOD Superman pictured!

LEARNING THE SUPERMAN!

1. Slide your feet off the pedals as soon as the bike leaves the lip of the ramp. Push the bike in front of you and upward. Straighten your arms. Hang on to the bike!

2. Pull your feet together and straighten them out to the back of the bike. Your body should be flat at this point, like you are lying down. The bike should be out in front of you.

3. Pull your feet back up to the bike and find the pedals.

4. Make sure you are coming in level, and adjust the bike if not.

5. Land smoothly and in control!

SUPERMAN

The Superman is one of the most readily recognized freestyle BMX air tricks. While in the air, the rider lifts both feet off the pedals and pushes them back behind him, parallel to the ground, resembling Superman flying. Some say it dates back to 1987, but others say it has been around informally as long as the sport itself.

To master the Superman, you need to be comfortable approaching your jumps at good speeds and be able to get decent height on your jumps.

NITRO METER

KEY FACTS

You need to be back on the seat with your feet on the pedals before landing. Otherwise, you're crashing!

Some riders can even let go of the bike completely for a few seconds, and this is called the Superman Nothing!

The pros add on other tricks while performing the Superman in order to maximize their scores and for the wow factor.

SUPERMAN SEAT GRAB

The Superman seat grab is when the rider takes his or her hands off the handlebars and grabs the seat while extending the body before grabbing back onto the bars and landing! It's even trickier than the traditional Superman!

FLIPPING WITH FLAIR
BACK, FRONT, AND DOUBLES!

Flips, an advanced skill, are when the rider and the bike turn head over heels while airborne.

There are many types of flips: backflip, frontflip, bikeflip, and flair are some examples. When you're learning these awesome moves, it's best to start with a foam pit or funbox.

PYRAMID

A pyramid is a bike or skate ramp that has a box in the middle with a flat top and ramps on two or more sides. These are great for learning tricks before progressing to a full skate park.

THE FAMILY OF FLIPS

FRONTFLIP

The hardest of the basic flips, the frontflip is all about the initial momentum. Using brakes can make it easier to get the proper surge. Practice it in a foam pit to begin with!

BACKFLIP

An advanced trick but much easier than the frontflip. As you take off from the jump, lean your head back. Always keep your head leaning back to nail the landing.

PRO TIPS

NITRO CIRCUS
TRAVIS PASTRANA

The pros add on other tricks while performing flips in order to maximize their scores. Flip combos include backflip barspin, double backflip, double frontflip, and more! Nitro Circus athlete Ryan Williams landed the world's first triple frontflip on a BMX in 2015.

FORWARD FRONT BIKEFLIP

A pro trick where the rider comes off the bike, flips only the bike in midair, and then returns back to the seat and pedals before landing.

FLAIR

A combination of a backflip and a 180-degree spin. Master the backflip before you try this more difficult trick! Flairs can only be performed on a quarter pipe.

WHIPPING, NOT FLIPPING
GET READY TO WHIP THAT TAIL

TAILWHIP

The tailwhip is an advanced trick where you spin the frame of the bike around you in a complete circle.

Your feet come off the bike, and you use the handlebars and your weight to turn the bike around in a circle. Your hands never leave the handlebars, as that is the axis of the spin. You move the handlebars in a tight circular motion to force the bike around your body.

The 360 tailwhip is a super difficult variation that includes a 360-degree spin while in the air.

NITRO METER

BEGINNER · INTERMEDIATE · ADVANCED · CRAZY

PRO TIPS

NITRO CIRCUS
ANDY BUCKWORTH

If you're ready to learn the tailwhip, start by spinning the frame on the ground first, so you can feel how the bike will move around its axis. Always look at your bike while you do this trick!

TRICK #16

BACKFLIP TAILWHIP

The backflip tailwhip is a backflip combined with a tailwhip. This is an advanced trick. The more air you get, the better!

NITRO METER

BEGINNER · INTERMEDIATE · ADVANCED · NITRO

PRO TIPS

NITRO CIRCUS
MATTY WHYATT

The pros make combos out of these already tricky tricks, such as the 360 tailwhip, the bunny hop tailwhip, the opposite tailwhip, the downside tailwhip, and the fakie tailwhip. Once you master a trick, you can make it look even cooler by adding barspins, bunny hops, and more!

DECADE

With this advanced trick, you throw yourself straight up off the bike at the height of the jump, position your body above the bike, and turn 360 degrees around the frame while holding the handlebars. You come around to meet the bike and land back on the pedals. The rider is spinning around, not the bike.

When you pop off the bike at the start, begin to spin as if you're doing a 360. As soon as you are in the air and rotating, kick the frame or push off the pedal in the opposite direction to the way you are spinning. Then rotate around the bike and wait for the bike to come underneath you before putting your feet back on the pedals to land.

NITRO METER

BEGINNER INTERMEDIATE ADVANCED

PRO TIPS

When learning this trick, make sure that once you are spinning and have kicked off the frame, you need to keep your legs together and be patient to wait for the pedals to come to you. Don't reach for them too early or the rotation will stop!

NITRO CIRCUS
TODD MEYN

PASTRANALAND: DREAMS BECOME REALITY

THE ULTIMATE ACTION SPORTS PLAYGROUND!

Travis Pastrana, famed motor sports and motocross freestyle racer and multiple X Games gold winner, built this incredible BMX compound on his 65-acre property in his home state of Maryland.

Many of the courses are deep in the woods, with a multitude of ramps and hills to choose from.

Pastranaland also has a colossal training complex for extreme athletes and stunt performers. It's chock-full of half-pipes, ramps of all shapes and sizes, a pit filled with foam cubes, a private skate park, and a fleet of off-road vehicles.

All sorts of pros are invited here by Travis to learn, play, and fly! In fact, several pros have set records at Pastranaland, including Josh Sheehan (the first triple backflip) and Jed Mildon (the first quad backflip). Special ramps and dirt setups were built just for these attempts!

NITRO CIRCUS WORLD FIRSTS!

PULLING OFF THE QUAD BACKFLIP: THE IMPOSSIBLE MADE POSSIBLE

Nitro Circus, led by ringleader Travis Pastrana, pushes the boundaries of action sports every day. Nitro Circus athletes travel the world performing tricks that have never been done before, including the world's first BMX quad backflip!

Some Nitro Circus world firsts include the first BMX double frontflip tailwhip, the BMX triple frontflip, and the FMX triple backflip that Josh Sheehan pulled in 2015.

In May 2015, Jed Mildon did what many riders thought was impossible and landed a BMX quad backflip! Dubbed "Revolution Day," Jed Mildon and James Foster battled head-to-head to see who could perform the world's first BMX quad backflip at Pastranaland, with Jed completing the trick first.

The Nitro Circus crew build special ramps and courses for their athletes to help them smash records and make their dreams come true!

RACIN', RAGIN', ROARIN' RAMPS

THE NITRO CIRCUS GIGANTA RAMP IS THE KING OF RAMPS!

Nitro Circus's famed Giganta ramp is a 50-foot ramp that, incredibly, tours with the athletes all over the world to help them pull off the craziest and most jaw-dropping stunts ever seen.

From recliners to boogie boards to Jet Skis and, of course, BMX bikes, everything has been tricked off the Giganta ramp!

The top of the Giganta ramp is a daunting place to be. It takes lots of practice before athletes build the confidence to perform incredible tricks off this monster of a ramp!

Dropping in on the Giganta ramp takes courage. After climbing the 70 steps to the top, athletes will then reach speeds of more than 35 mph before hitting a kicker that will launch them more than 25 feet into the air.

Nitro Circus and Travis Pastrana believe strongly in "progression through safety," which means when you're learning a new trick, you start with foam pits, resi ramps and landers, and/or inflatable landers. Nitro Circus builds safety into all of their ramps!

NITRO BIKE CONTRAPTIONS

NITRO CIRCUS RAMPS UP THE SHENANIGANS!

The Nitro Circus worldwide tour features Travis Pastrana and the other Nitro Circus athletes pushing the envelope during every performance!

The tour showcases the best athletes in BMX, who ramp up the shenanigans with the greatest, most ridiculous, funniest show in Nitro history. Bigger ramps, crazier stunts, better jumps, and even some rough landings—it's all part of their worldwide tour. This collection of outrageous contraptions tops the bill!

During the two-hour Nitro Circus show, the riders jump just about anything to entertain the crowd and just have fun, including this beach cruiser with a baby carrier attached (no baby included)!

The tall bike is a favorite with the crowd. It's basically two bikes welded together to create the sketchiest bicycle in the world! Riders can't even touch the ground when they are on the bike, which makes getting off the bike just as hard as backflipping it.

Contraptions they have jumped during their shows include lounge chairs, tandem tricycles, wheelbarrows, and even hospital gurneys! These silly minibikes are a favorite with the crowd, and the riders perform all sort of tricks on them, including backflips.

The penny-farthing bike is another fun contraption that Nitro Circus uses to wow and entertain the crowd during tours. Riders push the envelope and showcase these crazy-looking bikes with all kinds of fantastic stunts.

TANDEM RIDING
DOUBLE THE ACTION

Sometimes a single-person backflip isn't hard enough for Nitro Circus athletes, and they attempt backflips with two, or sometimes three, people on one bike!

Defying gravity and physics is just part of the fun, like with this stupendous two-person backflip! They've even pulled off a backflip with four people on a motocross bike... Who knows what they'll try next!

EVERYTHING FLIES

The last thing you would expect to see 25 feet in the air is a regular old road bike. These are made for speed and not air! But there is no rulebook at Nitro Circus and everything, even a road bike, can fly.

CONTRAPTIONS STEAL THE SHOW!

THE NITRO CIRCUS SHOW IS STUPID FUN

During the Nitro Circus show, Nitro Circus athletes like Brandon Schmidt, Dusty Wygle, Aaron "Crum" Sauvage, and Ethen Roberts ride and jump all sorts of crazy contraptions to wow the crowd.

You name it, and they will try to ride it! Sometimes they land it, sometimes they don't, but it's always hilarious fun for the crowd!

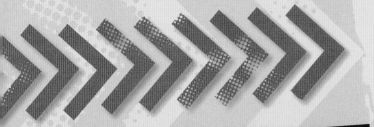

YOU RIDE IT, YOU JUMP IT!

Nitro Circus athletes have been known to ride and flip just about anything on wheels for the fun of it and to entertain their fans. This includes skis, tandem tricycles, Barbie cars, a mini VW Bus, lounge chairs, wheelbarrows, kid-sized Big Wheels, shopping carts, rocking horses with wheels, boogie boards, bobsleds, Jet Skis, skateboards, and even hospital gurneys!

You never know what you will see fly at a Nitro Circus show. Dusty Wygle is the world's only land boogie boarder!

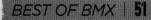

SPOTLIGHT ON
ANDY BUCKWORTH

DATE OF BIRTH: February 4, 1990
HOMETOWN: Lake Haven, AUS

Aussie Andy Buckworth is a BMX legend who made a name for himself in 2010 when he became the second athlete ever to land a double frontflip on a BMX bike. Andy went on to punch his "world's first" card when he added some flare to the double frontflip, injecting a Superman variation into the mix!

As a world-renowned competitor and accomplished park rider, it's no wonder Buckworth has been riding with Nitro Circus from the beginning.

SUPERMAN DOUBLE FRONTFLIP

WORLD'S FIRST

NITRO METER

BEGINNER · INTERMEDIATE · ADVANCED · CRAZY!

NITRO CIRCUS
SPOTLIGHT ON
JAIE TOOHEY

DATE OF BIRTH: May 6, 1991
HOMETOWN: Lake Munmorah, AUS

Like many athletes in Nitro Circus, Jaie Toohey got his start in racing but quickly found that while speed and intense racing are rewarding, he was more drawn to the inverted world of freestyle.

The Newcastle, Australia, native made the transition to the park and ramps and has been wowing crowds ever since. Toohey has scored podium finishes in renowned competitions across the globe, including Nitro World Games and Dew Tour, and is always looking to try something new and impressive as he tours the world with the Nitro Circus crew.

WORLD'S FIRST
BACKFLIP TRIPLE TAILWHIP

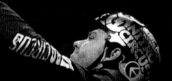

NITRO CIRCUS
SPOTLIGHT ON
MATTY WHYATT

DATE OF BIRTH: July 11, 1991
HOMETOWN: Geelong, AUS

As one of Nitro Circus's exciting BMX riders, Matt "Matty" Whyatt is continually pushing boundaries with his explosive jumps and bold new tricks.

Whyatt got into BMX after first trying skating and then taking up surfing. Fittingly a *Sons of Anarchy* fan, the Geelong, Australia, native's achievements include creating his signature "Whyatt Riot," which took more than four years of attempts before he perfected the move. The Whyatt Riot is a backflip tailwhip to late 360. Matty also landed the first ever doublewhip to barspin and would like to add a second whip to the backflip tailwhip to late 360. "If you fail, try, try, and try again," he says.

WORLD'S FIRST

THE WHYATT RIOT

NITRO METER

NITRO CIRCUS
SPOTLIGHT ON
TODD MEYN

DATE OF BIRTH: November 23, 1995
HOMETOWN: Perth, AUS

BMX sensation Todd Meyn has spent countless hours perfecting his craft. Growing up in Perth, Australia, if you were looking for Todd as a youngster, you could surely find him at the skate park.

At age 15, Todd placed second in his first professional competition, and many more followed. With a résumé full of impressive tricks and a fun-loving attitude, Todd made his way up the ranks and was offered a spot on the Nitro Circus crew.

WORLD'S FIRST DOUBLE FRONTFLIP TAILWHIP

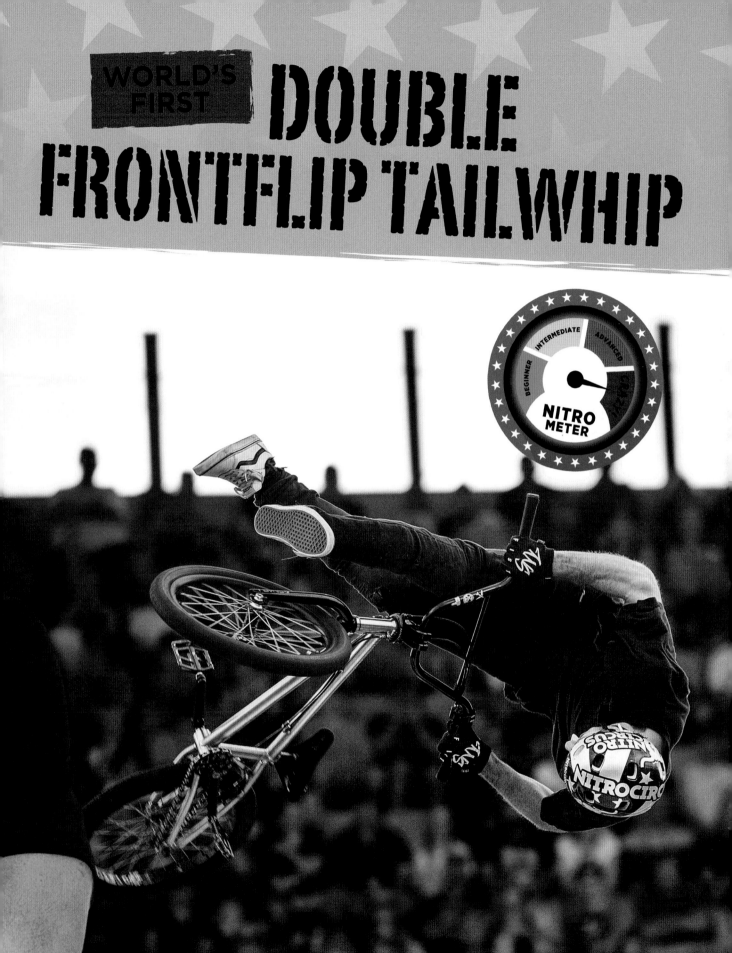

NITRO METER

BEGINNER INTERMEDIATE ADVANCED

SPOTLIGHT ON
KURTIS DOWNS

DATE OF BIRTH: March 25, 1992
HOMETOWN: Firth, ID

Idaho native Kurtis Downs is one of the most dynamic and innovative BMX riders in the sport. Despite keeping a relatively low profile, his talent often precedes him.

Downs earned podium finishes at both Nitro World Games and at his first-ever X Games. Keep an eye out for this BMXer with FMX style. Much of his riding is influenced by his early beginnings in moto, including his FMX-inspired world's first—the BMX stripper flip.

BACKFLIP QUADRUPLE TAILWHIP

NITRO METER

BEGINNER INTERMEDIATE ADVANCED

THE UNIVERSITY OF UTAH

NITRO CIRCUS

SPOTLIGHT ON
RYAN WILLIAMS

DATE OF BIRTH: June 22, 1994
HOMETOWN: Sunshine Coast, AUS

Born and raised on Australia's Sunshine Coast, Ryan "R-Willy" Williams had a passion for action sports from a young age. R-Willy had dreams of becoming a fighter pilot or an astronaut, always wanting to push the limits on what is possible.

R-Willy is one the most versatile and exciting individuals to watch in action sports. With countless world's first tricks tied to his name (such as the first triple backflip on a scooter), Ryan has amassed quite the fanbase (including more than 1 million followers on Instagram).

In 2018, R-Willy took 1st place in X Games Sydney with a nothing front bikeflip followed by a frontflip flair.

WORLD'S FIRST **TRIPLE FRONTFLIP**

NITRO METER

BEGINNER INTERMEDIATE ADVANCED

NITRO CIRCUS

Vice President, Licensing & Publishing Amanda Joiner
Editorial Manager Carrie Bolin

Editor Jessica Firpi
Designer Luis Fuentes
Text Kezia Endsley
Proofreader Rachel Paul
Reprographics Bob Prohaska
Special Thanks to Ripley's Cartoonist, John Graziano

President Andy Edwards
Chief Commercial Officer Brett Clarke
**Vice President, Global Licensing &
  Consumer Products** Cassie Dombrowski
Vice President, Creative Dov Ribnick
Global Director, Public Relations Reid Vokey
Director, Digital Content Marketing Charley Daniels
**Global Accounts & Activation Manager,
  Consumer Products** Andrew Hogan
Art Director & Graphic Designer Joshua Geduld
Contributor Micah Kranz

For more information regarding permission, contact:
VP Licensing & Publishing
Ripley Entertainment Inc.
7576 Kingspointe Parkway, Suite 188
Orlando, Florida 32819
Email: publishing@ripleys.com
www.ripleys.com/books

Manufactured in China in May 2019.
First Printing

Library of Congress Control Number: 2019933265

PUBLISHER'S NOTE
While every effort has been made to verify the accuracy of the entries in this book, the Publisher cannot be held responsible for any errors contained in the work. They would be glad to receive any information from readers.

WARNING
Some of the stunts and activities are undertaken by experts and should not be attempted by anyone without adequate training and supervision.

PHOTO CREDITS

2-3 (dp) © MarcelClemens/Shutterstock.com; **3** (tr) Photography by Nate Christenson, (br) Photography by Mark Watson; **4** (bl) sampics/Corbis via Getty Images, (br) David Berding/Icon Sportswire via Getty Images; **4-5** (dp) Photography by Mark Watson; **5** (bl) Photography by Andre Nordheim, (br) Photography by Mark Watson; **7** (r) Photography by Kevin Conners; **8-9** (dp) © Perry Harmon/Shutterstock.com; **10** attl via Getty Images/iStockphoto; **11** totalphoto/Alamy Stock Photo; **16-17** (dp) Richard Bord/Getty Images; **18** (bl) Photography by Mark Watson; **19** (br) © FADEDinkDesigns/Shutterstock.com; **20** (b) Courtesy of Ripley Cartoonist, John Graziano; **22** Charles Knox-Creative/Alamy Stock Photo; **23** Keith Morris/Alamy Stock Photo; **25** (t) Photography by Kevin Conners; **26** © s-ts/Shutterstock.com; **27** (b) Photography by Kevin Conners; **28** Photography by Mark Watson; **29** (l) Photography by Mark Watson; **30** (l) Photography by Mark Watson; **31** (l) Photography by Mark Watson; **32** (b) Photography by Mark Watson; **32-33** (dp) james vaughan-spencer/Alamy Stock Photo; **33** (b) Photography by Mark Watson; **34** (bl, br) Photography by Mark Watson; **34-35** (dp) Photography by Mark Watson; **35** (tr) Cate Norian Koch/Red Bull Content Pool, (bl) Photography by Mark Watson, (br) Photography by Kevin Conners; **36** (b) Photography by Mark Watson; **36-37** (dp) Photography by Chris Tedesco; **38** Photography by Mark Watson; **39** Photography by Mark Watson; **40** (tr) Cate Norian Koch/Red Bull Content Pool , (bl) Photography by Nate Christenson; **40-41** (dp) Photography by Nate Christenson; **44-45** © Sport the library/Brett Stanley; **45** (cr) Photography by Nate Christenson, (cr) Photography by Mark Watson; **46** (bc) Photography by Mark Watson; **46-47** (dp) Photography by Mark Watson; **47** (tr, br) Photography by Mark Watson; **48-49** (dp) Photography by Mark Watson; **49** (tr, br) Photography by Mark Watson; **51** (tr, cr, br) Photography by Mark Watson; **53** © Sport the library/Jeff Crow; **55** Photography by Chris Tedesco; **57** Photography by Chris Tedesco; **59** Photography by Mark Watson; **MASTER GRAPHICS** Nitro Meter: Created by Luis Fuentes

Special Thanks to   Bell Sports, Inc., FIST Handwear PTY Ltd., Greenover Ltd., Hyper Bicycles, Inc.

Key: t = top, b = bottom, c = center, l = left, r = right, sp = single page, dp = double page, bkg = background

All other photos are from Nitro Circus. Every attempt has been made to acknowledge correctly and contact copyright holders, and we apologize in advance for any unintentional errors or omissions, which will be corrected in future editions.